JABEZ INCARNATE

Joladé Olusanya

Out-Spoken Press
London

Published by Out-Spoken Press,
PO Box 78744
London, N11 9FG

All rights reserved
© Joladé Olusanya

The rights of Joladé Olusanya to be identified as the author of this work have been asserted by them in accordance with section 77 of the Copyright, Designs and Patents Act 1988.

A CIP record for this title is available from the British Library.

This book is in copyright. Subject to statutory exception and to provisions of relevant collective licensing agreements, no reproduction of any part may take place without the written permission of Out-Spoken Press.

First edition published 2025
ISBN: 9781068671272

Typeset in Futura and Adobe Caslon
Design by Patricia Ferguson
Cover image ©Joladé Olusanya
Printed and bound by Print Resources

Out-Spoken Press is supported using public funding by the National Lottery through Arts Council England.

JABEZ INCARNATE

CONTENTS

I PACK LIGHT	1
LET ME TELL YOU HOW TO BUILD CHARACTER	2
SANGO-IN-WAITING	3
THE GOSPEL ACCORDING TO MAN LIIKKEEE…	5
LIGHT METER	6
A RECIPE FOR LONGING	7
WHEN I SAY I'M WAITING	8
PRUNING	9
EVERYTHING ABOUT ME ENDS	10
ON THE 253	11
PENTECOST	12
WHAT'S IN MY NAME?	13
KAREEM ONCE SAID, 'I AM A WALKING GUNFINGER…'	15
QUICK MATHS	16
HOW WE DIE	17
HOME TRAINING	18
I THINK I WANT TO WAIT	19

*

NOTES	21
ACKNOWLEDGEMENTS	23

The block still don't know us
Can't pronounce the name / but they will miss us when we go

—Lex Amor

I PACK LIGHT

do laundry before I leave
clothes cushion the things that break
the house keys go in first
and come out last
I arrive four hours early
eat enough to induce the itis pre-flight
I watch the tarmac and wonder
why the world's gateways aren't more peng
a plane is a thing of awe
guesswork turned engineering
a facade that believes in itself
we sit inside its confidence
but are full of none
uncertainty can fleece a pocket
it's attractive because it makes you like the idea
of going somewhere
but you can only plan that far
travel is a luxury
it takes clearing a schedule
you do it if you're brave enough to.

LET ME TELL YOU HOW TO BUILD CHARACTER

make home a stranger
less names
more honorifics
abbreviate your mother
have a steel bed frame for a chiropractor
feed on the unripe
soak overnight
praise a God you don't feel
clap
see parent days as visitation hours
carry water like your life depends on it
grow callouses then callous
let iron swing you around
call it gains if you live
get colonised by soldier ants
dance for rain
sleep when you can't
have a roster of friends turned exes
own a can opener
use public transport
learn the smell of kerosene and petrol
clap
talk to God in public anyway

SANGO-IN-WAITING

> *'Every step I took yesterday walking away as men of @PoliceNG shot at me I braced myself for the moment of impact ... #EndSars'*
> — Aisha Yesufu, October 11 2020

this is how to make a man
clear his throat with a gun.

become my mother
cumulonimbus pregnant with Yorùbá hail
steering through Lagos heat with no air con.

she tells a policeman: *say 'ehn' again idiot!*
and becomes bulletproof.
it was the double-glazed crack in his eyes for me. in the backseat I
learn my only use
for this tongue.

I cannot rain like my mother.

I just witness from far.
                         backup cloud
for a toll gate camera.
I see blood.
I hear guns, remember phlegm.
I see men make an auction house out of a street.

I see time still a body.
photoshop deaths.
blue cascading
         Helvetica
                Neue
obituaries.

I want to rain but I'm all character
limits, stratus clouds,
drafts pivoting between protest, witch-hunt,
late invoices

all the things we became just to say
we are here – a soft clearing
of the throat.
        thunder fire you
                still.

THE GOSPEL ACCORDING TO MAN LIIKKEEE...

And God said let there be light then light said let everything I touch have shadow shape and function then function said let man skank wheel up riddims bogle see other man in the dance see kin not threat forget Cozzie Livs call up Mumsie tell her I love you like fire loves yam like yam loves designer egg like how warm coco bread folds over flaky cheesy beef patties breaking is okay here my G you're okay here good here you her them man come sit fam stretch cross legs don't watch face or door it's calm outside good outside like when good sun hits skin like when pollen's not an opp grind food not teeth unclench jaw free the grief in your fist spud me with the resonance that will tell my heir he's good too God said let there be light then I asked God to give man shades discs on eyes that contour face so a man can't tell if man's eyes are smiling if man's pupils are dilated like pupils in school cos man didn't learn nothing except that man didn't learn so God teach man something so man can do something cos man wants to do something still.

LIGHT METER*

f/22   I stain the page and a day is done.

f/16   a father and son stand bluffing but one doesn't know how.

f/11   in the sun's setting there's grain, contrast and blacks.

f/8   I'm saying rebellion requires colour correction.

f/5.6   a shelf of poetry says my corner of the world is progressive.

f/4   this is me pulling a poem from a blur.

f/3.5   a poem has the privilege of being incoherent.

f/2.8   I think I'm pensive until I see how fog sits on a day.

f/2   all I want is to write with the audacity of white people.

f/1.8   I'm lying.

f/1.4   I just want their audacity.

---

*   an instrument for measuring the intensity of light, used to mainly to show the correct exposure when taking a photograph

A RECIPE FOR LONGING

It's October. I'm in a Manhattan diner eating spaghetti bolognese that's really just bolognese featuring spaghetti. I order black coffee made sweet by one of the many brands of sweeteners America has at its disposal. We are spoilt for choice in all the ways we can show kindness in the world but don't. I'm thinking about what I need to live in this city. Grit, grace, multiple sources of warmth and equal amounts of cool. This city gives much and requires it too and I, with my traveling-man self, feel like I know it well enough to say it has taken a toll on me now and the me I will be tomorrow. Here, the day is when you fight for space. Night is when you remember you have too much of it. I find a diner. Slide into a booth that gives me a view of the entrance and expectation. Order what makes me feel like I carry depth. Drink what makes me procrastinate the need to sleep. Coffee is the colour of the realities I run from. Now I'm awake long enough to face them. This is a recipe for romanticising longing. The kind that makes you sit in diners at midnight. New York is where you go to make your loneliness cinematic. Where you hunch yourself over mugs, food, anything that lets heat touch you like the hands you want. Everyone in a diner is the same – there for the kind of warmth you can buy and get refills for at no extra cost. Where lovers are foreign sauced-stained aprons who pour into your cup without asking because they know it's empty. I post solo views online. People envy my lens. Call me cinematographer. As if I intended to paint with light. They save my post in folders marked: *flights not feelings*. But it's both. Even now in this diner, I am coming and going between what I should feel and where I should go. People save my posts. They DM and ask how I managed to get the grain so fine. Colours right. Lighting perfect. I don't know. But I'll make up a reason if it keeps us talking.

WHEN I SAY I'M WAITING

what I mean is breaking
doesn't always make a sound

I am not reserved   just sitting
still   this is where rejection
and promise meet

what I'm saying is
here is a composed way to end

PRUNING

the mandem are softest
where Jesus is a man

touching a blade to our temples
and throats ridding us of the unruly
growth that comes with living

this service we gladly attend
salvation worth every tithe

when we leave
do you not see the glory of God
shine clean from our faces?

EVERYTHING ABOUT ME ENDS

with jazz or just ends
maybe jazz is a sweet
interlude in my debut EP of a life

jazz is here
but if I can't find it
in a flat black wax circle
I'll find it where I'm a stranger
in tongue and pace only

where I swell and lean
in all the ways jazz does

where the sun doesn't steal
glances of me between buildings

where we frolic in water like children
do through verdant fields

maybe jazz is water
a thing only God can write

how else do you explain
the perfect randomness of a ripple?

ON THE 253

A drunk white guy shouts at me: *You have hair like my grandfather!* I said: *Cool.* A boy ahead of me spat in the face of his mother. He forgot that he'd soon be home where no one could save him. A man comes upstairs and the boy says to him: Hi Uncle Robert! Reunions and coincidences are only this convenient in things you can write. Drunk white guy belches out loud and says: *Pardon me!* The bus stops. Three white boys in hoodies politicking outside a crumbling block get on. They look like they were discussing world hunger. I'm sure they were. Drunk white guy shouts at a Rasta saying: *My stepdad is Jamaican too!* When drunk white guy says: *My mother is Irish!* Rasta smiles gold teeth because his great-grandfather was too. Drunk white guy says: *There's good and bad in everybody!* Then: *I'm trying to reach my drug dealer!* The bus stops again. Drunk white guy gets off saying: *Stay bless brudda!* Rasta responds: *Keep it cool!* I'm trying. Honest to God I'm trying.

PENTECOST

some nights I'm taller than my bed
my feet touch the edge of worry
I know what it means to carry over

there's not enough J Dilla in the world
for all the melancholy I am

Jabez incarnate
named in a way that forced me to God

I too am a magician
pulling poems out of misdirection

I don't take wrong turns
ask my mother
I rode shotgun from early

my siblings watched TV
I watched where we were going

I'm still going
now with more feeling than sight

like grandma dancing in her hospital ward
in front of her junior wives

she was going where their curses couldn't
        touch her anymore
she'd be the first again

WHAT'S IN MY NAME?

consequence, spoilers
the socks my father didn't pull up

in my second name
my mother's chance

to be tied to me again   eternal umbilical cord
across the distances I'd put between us

the type I can only cut via deed poll
estrangement you can't come back from

in my last name
praise and pleads

every time a man says it wrong
I become an import

the heavens frown
God clears His throat

somewhere in my lineage a son flips a table
sending milk, honey, ideas of western plenty flying

I wrote this halfway through brushing my teeth
gums stained with the attempt of a fresh start

my tongue has said my names
in all the accents it's been stewed in

curling every way round their subtexts
most of our names are abbreviations

we live our lives hoping we complete them
by the time we die

what's in my name?
say it right

see the surprise in my face
a blessing;

for once I am called
like I belong

KAREEM ONCE SAID,
'I AM A WALKING GUNFINGER...'

now you know how we survived

we walked with smoke
learnt how to be fire

target-practiced on potential opps
before we left yard

what weapon would dare prosper
against men with wicked skanks like these?

us who skanked
at the back of the bus
on the corner in the clash
shubz football cage
playground chicken shop

if you still don't get it
we were shadow boxing in sets

eights sixteens thirty-twos
with wheel ups for a buzzer

baptised by sweat
brilliant equaliser of men

QUICK MATHS

To work out the square root of eternity
I look in the mirror and do the math.

Now is where you and I can't be anything
but what we are. Though inside we hope

we'll be enough for tomorrow and each other
the day after and the versions of each

other we'll be then. I like being above ground.
I jump on anything that lets me see the sky

and the sun on your face. Anything that gives
you the glow you have in my mind.

True say I'm the best poet when I leave
my house. All the prompts I need come

fill the gaps in my day. Not every poem
needs an ending but I'm thinking of mine.

I want my life to be something loved ones know
off-head. Like "to be or not to be?" but less of

a question because I was here and still will be
every time you recite me or my name.

In my land a name is a prayer so say it like
you know God answers those. We don't

twist tongues for bants. It's the way
the Spirit told us we were made to talk.

HOW WE DIE

bro you were all uniform
I was watching a knife
making its daily debut
still learning its lines

its owner was one of the reasons
Mum said not to walk
through the estate
I watched a man's squire sponsor

death from a distance
but my voice rose
to meet his and I witnessed
the birth of a testimony

running to where
it would be embargoed
until Sunday service
you don't remember cos

you weren't supposed to see
blood outside a body
you don't remember cos
I was more shield than brother

I kept many things from you
and sometimes I think
I was too good at that

HOME TRAINING

I'm closest to my mother
only when asking how to cook

in those moments she ignores
that I look nothing like my culture

maybe she thinks:
even if he does not marry—
bí mo ṣe ní láti ṣe
he will feed his home—
bí mo ṣe ní ifẹ si

one auntie told me:
máà mu obìnrin aláwọ̀ funfun wá'lé!

my mother is indifferent
I think

if family meant shared opinions
there'd be more complete ones

mine has the bone density of my late grandfather
shaking from every little thing

once in a while I sub out my mirror
for my mother's eyes

if she keeps my gaze then I know
I look a lot less like her fears

I THINK I WANT TO WAIT

before naming my child
give time for some of the *ings* and *isms*

to show before assuming them into being
God knew us before we were born

I who is still trying to know who that is
have no business playing Him to another like me

assuming a stance I haven't seen
in my country they call names prayers

mine feels like a second chance for my parents
I think they want me to fix something

we should wait a lifetime
before naming children

give them a minute to exist
their eyes time to adjust to light

so they can see us in its glory
and know what not to become

NOTES

'sango-in-waiting' was first published in *Poetry London*, Issue 100, Autumn 2021.

'let me tell you how to build character' and 'I Pack Light' are forthcoming in *The Poetry Review*, Summer 2025.

ACKNOWLEDGEMENTS

Thank you to…

Catherine Labiran and Nat Nye. XII Talents forever.

Jemilea Wisdom-Baako, Peter Kahn, R. A. Villanueva, Jacob Sam-La Rose, Rachel Long, Tolu Agbelusi, Nick Makoha, Malika Booker, Jill Abram, Inua Ellams, Natalie 'Floacist' Stewart, Nathalie Teitler, Jasmine Mans, Mr. Gee, Roger Robinson for all the encouragement, guidance and then some.

SXWKS, my eternal circumference: Lex Amor, Caleb Femi, Charles, Keziah, Aiden, Naya, Josette, Kush, Sarah Aluko, Julian Knxx, Michael, Olivia, Flo, Idowu, Theresa Lola, Dillon, Haja, Rui, Remi, Marta, Abu, et al.

Kelewele Mandem: Moses, Robert and Peter.

My g's dem: Nezyah, Sia and Cecil.

Yomi Ṣode for more than words will ever convey. Shout out 10K for the healthy gas.

Obsidian Group E: Ariana Benson, Courtney Conrad, Be Manzini, Peter deGraft-Johnson, Len Lawson, Raina León, Keri Mosuro, Tanatsei Gambura, especially Alexa Patrick.

Gboyega Odubanjo, Kareem Parkins-Brown, Raymond Antrobus, Jeremiah Brown, Gabriel Àkámó, Hibaq Osman, Gabriel Jones, Amina Jama, Tania, Sumia Juxun, Jade Benn, Shania Akilah, Zara Sheikh, Troy Cabida, JJ Bola, Emmanuel Sugo, Shadé Joseph, LionHeart, Tobi Kyeremateng, Aliyah Hasinah, Ofem Ubi (the Great), Lord Michael Hastings, Hatice, Intalekt, Haroon, Juwad, James Massiah, Sophia Thakur, Victor Azubuike, Jody, Jamal, Sean Mahoney, Jay O, Tomisin Adepeju, Malakai, Tasneim, Jumi, Kiraya, Belinda Zhawi, Mateki-san, Bianca Vivion, Deji Thomas, Delores, Aisling Fahey, Assumpta Vitcu, Dekan Apajee, YAC, PK Gen,

MoP, Amos Bursary, CB and Anchor of Hope.

The Poetry Review, *bath magg*, *Poetry London*, Writerz & Scribez, Jawdance, Boxed-In, Flo Vortex, Sofar Sounds, Southbank Centre, Born:Free, Nuyorican Poets Café, G.A.S. Foundation, The Orange Room Collective, Vocals & Verses, The Albany, R.A.P Party, every poetry night, community and publishing house.

St. Aloysius' Class of '07, Ms Mauris-Blanc, wherever you are. Miss Whyte RIP.

Anthony Anaxagorou, Patricia Ferguson and the Out-Spoken Press team.

My G, Afaron, for pushing me into the light that night at uni. Lequan for doing the same in Gambia.

Ryan for letting me take your portrait. Pink Folder Film Lab for processing and the community. Nate for the constant support. Daniel for the brotherhood.

Everyone who's ever reached out in person or virtually to show love, put me on, give space, champion, challenge and journey with me.

The siblings, love always.

My mother, my genesis, thank you.

God, cos you reign.

And to you, for waiting.

From here, we go.

SELECTED OTHER TITLES BY OUT-SPOKEN PRESS

Almost, with Tenderness • MAYA CASPARI

I Sugar the Bones • JUANA ADCOCK

Down • REBECCA MCCUTCHEON

Bark, Archive Splinter • JAY GAO

Boiled Owls • AZAD ASHIM SHARMA

[...] • FADY JOUDAH

Vulgar Errors / Feral Subjects • FRAN LOCK

State of Play: Poets of East & Southeast Asian Heritage in Conversation • EDS. EDDIE TAY & JENNIFER WONG

Nude as Retrospect • ALEX MARLOW

Today Hamlet • NATALIE SHAPERO

G&T • OAKLEY FLANAGAN

sad thing angry • EMMA JEREMY

Trust Fall • WILLIAM GEE

Cane, Corn & Gully • SAFIYA KAMARIA KINSHASA

apricot • KATIE O'PRAY

Mother of Flip-Flops • MUKAHANG LIMBU

Dog Woman • HELEN QUAH

Caviar • SARAH FLETCHER

Somewhere Something is Burning • ALICE FRECKNALL

flinch & air • LAURA JANE LEE

Fetch Your Mother's Heart • LISA LUXX

Seder • ADAM KAMMERLING

54 Questions for the Man Who Sold a Shotgun to My Father • JOE CARRICK-VARTY

Lasagne • WAYNE HOLLOWAY-SMITH

Mutton Rolls • ARJI MANUELPILLAI

SELECTED OTHER TITLES BY OUT-SPOKEN PRESS

Contains Mild Peril • FRAN LOCK

Epiphaneia • RICHARD GEORGES

Stage Invasion: Poetry & the Spoken Word Renaissance • PETE BEARDER

The Neighbourhood • HANNAH LOWE

The Games • HARRY JOSEPHINE GILES

Songs My Enemy Taught Me • JOELLE TAYLOR

To Sweeten Bitter • RAYMOND ANTROBUS

How You Might Know Me • SABRINA MAHFOUZ

Heterogeneous, New & Selected Poems • ANTHONY ANAXAGOROU

Titanic • BRIDGET MINAMORE